Contents

Words printed in **bold** are explained in the glossary.

♥ What is a charity?

Have you ever thought what it would be like to have no home? Where would you sleep? How would you stay warm and dry? Where would you keep all your things?

Some charities provide warm clothes, food and beds for people who live on the streets.

These are the problems that face millions of homeless people in the world. Finding a home is very difficult when you have no money and no one to help you. Certain charities work hard to help homeless people solve these problems.

Charities sometimes provide homeless people with somewhere to sleep. They help homeless people to learn new skills so that they can get jobs. And they help people living in damp, cramped or run-down housing to find a better home.

This homeless person is pleased to be out of the cold and wet.

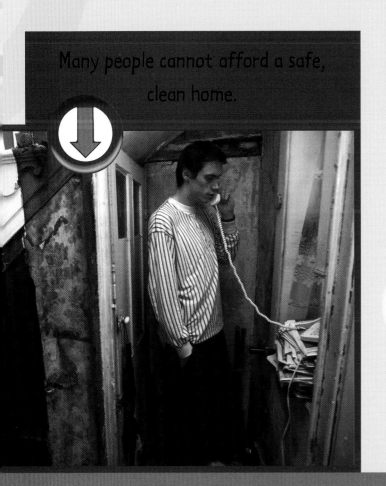

Many people cannot afford a safe, clean home.

What would you miss most if you didn't have a home?

On the streets

Have you ever seen someone sleeping in a shop doorway or in a train station? Probably you have, since many homeless people live in towns and cities.

Begging is the only way some homeless people can get money for food and drink.

People usually live on the streets because they have nowhere else to go. They may have no friends or family to stay with. They may also be ill or have a problem with drugs or alcohol.

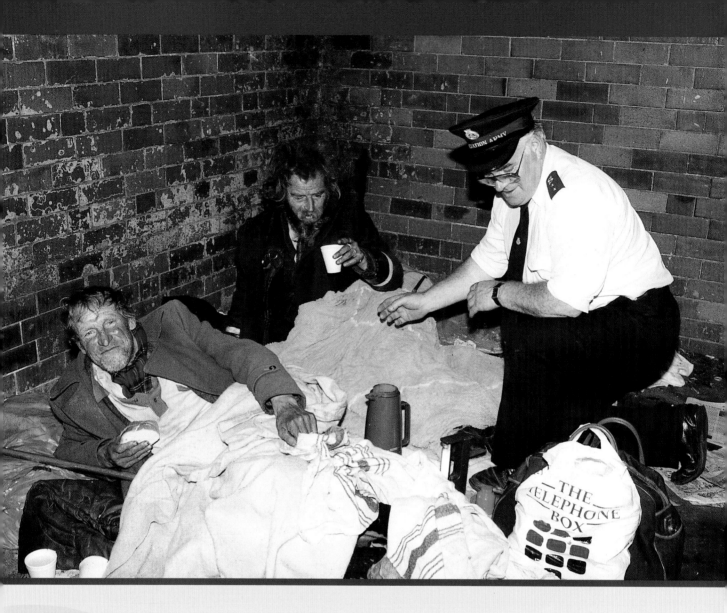

Every night Salvation Army
workers give out hot drinks
and food to people who
sleep on the streets.

How would you manage if you had no
family or friends to care for you?

♥ A place to stay

If you were forced to sleep outdoors one night, how would you feel in the morning? You would probably be tired, hungry and dirty, as well as cold and miserable.

CASE STUDY

Andrew ran away from home because his mother's boyfriend kept picking on him. The charity, Centrepoint, gave him a warm, safe room to stay in at one of its **hostels**.

Some charities run hostels for homeless people. Many of them have clean bedrooms, hot showers, good food and somewhere to wash clothes. Homeless people can feel better and get themselves clean.

The International Committee of the Red Cross provides tents, bedding and food parcels for people who have lost their homes because of war.

Around the world there are millions of people who do not have anywhere safe to sleep each night. Wars force many people to leave their homes.

What would you take with you if you had to leave home?

♥ Food

If you had no money, how could you afford to eat? Many charities and churches run day centres that give homeless people the chance to make friends over a hot, healthy meal.

These men are enjoying a meal in a day centre.

The Crisis FareShare scheme feeds thousands of homeless people.

Supermarkets throw away boxes and boxes of food that is no longer fresh enough to sell – even though it is still fresh enough to eat. Shops **donate** this food to the charity Crisis, so they can provide meals for homeless people.

In hot climates, homeless people very quickly become ill if they do not keep clean and eat proper food. The organisation UNICEF works around the world, handing out fresh food to stop homeless people getting sick.

These boxes of blankets and fruit have been sent to help refugees in Macedonia.

What should you eat every day to stay healthy?

When you feel ill, you know that if you rest and take any medicine you are given by the doctor, you should get well again.

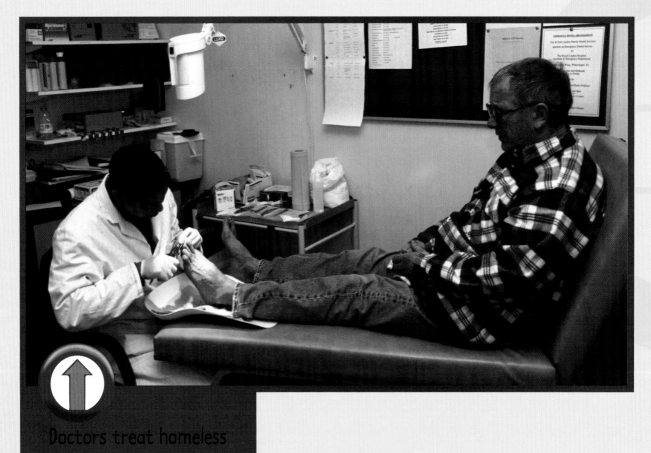

Doctors treat homeless people in special clinics.

Because homeless people do not have a warm, clean place to live, they are more likely to become ill. As a result, many homeless people do not live as long as other people.

St Mungo's is a charity that provides doctors who examine homeless people, making sure they get the help and medicines they need to get better.

Some people live in housing that is unhealthy and dangerous. This is because their homes are often damp. Also they do not have enough room to keep kettles, heaters and electrical wires out of the way, which can cause an accident.

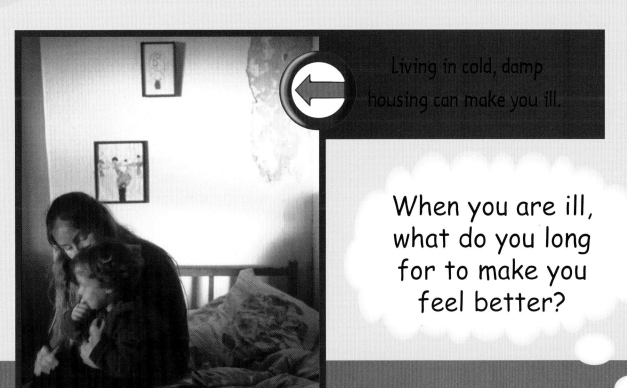

Living in cold, damp housing can make you ill.

When you are ill, what do you long for to make you feel better?

♥ Homeless children

Have you ever felt hurt or angry about something and wanted to run away from the problem? Well lots of children run away from home for this reason, only to discover that living on the streets is very frightening and lonely.

When you run away from home, you have no one to keep you out of danger.

The NSPCC provides a **refuge** for children who run away from home. The charity helps sort out problems so that the children can go back to their families or move to a new, happier home.

In Brazil, lots of children live on the streets because their families cannot afford to keep them. They have no one to protect them from harm. Jubilee Action provides a safe home for some of these children.

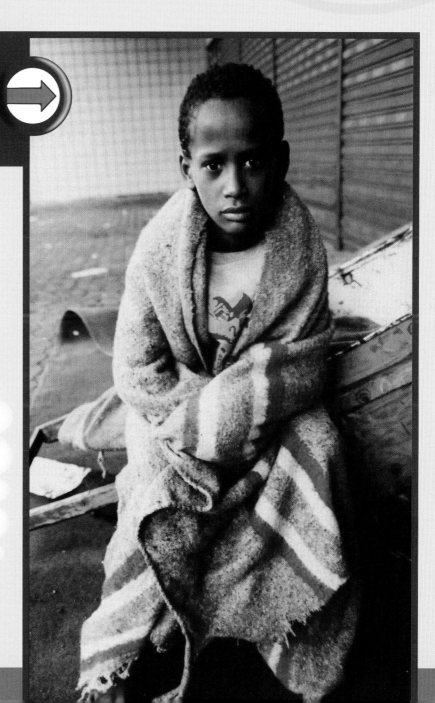

Many children in Brazil have no one to look after them.

What would frighten you most if you lived on the streets alone?

♥ Refugees

Imagine being forced to leave your home by men with guns because a war has started. How would you feel?

This happens to lots of people around the world. These people are known as **refugees**. Many are so scared that they move to a new country to feel safe.

Some people lose their homes in a war.

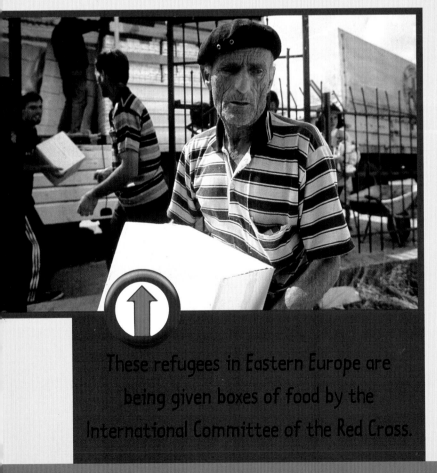

These refugees in Eastern Europe are being given boxes of food by the International Committee of the Red Cross.

Charities provide food and tents for refugees away from war areas. There, they can plan their return home or a new life in a different country.

The Refugee Council has taught this Vietnamese boy the language of his new country, so he can make friends and talk to people.

It can be a great shock arriving in a new country, where people speak a different language and do things in a different way.

Charities help refugees when they arrive in their new country until they feel more settled.

Where would you go if your family was forced to leave your home?

♥ Earning money

Have you ever wanted something really badly and saved your money to get it? Homeless people have little or no money to buy what they want or need.

Charities help homeless people get a job so that they have some money to buy things they need like clothes and food. Having work also makes it easier for a homeless person to find somewhere to live again.

Many homeless people sell The Big Issue magazine. For every magazine sold, the seller keeps about half the money.

THE BIG ISSUE

The old-school avenger versus the young pretenders

If a homeless person has not worked for a long time, it can be very hard to find a job.

Charities like Alone in London teach homeless young people to do things like use computers, so they can get work that pays enough to live on.

What would you do to earn money if you were homeless?

♥ Finding a home

Look in a newspaper and you will find a long list of empty houses and flats. You may wonder why homeless people don't live in them.

The reason is that they cost too much money. Homeless people, even those who have just found a job, cannot afford to buy or **rent** most of the empty houses and flats available.

Most towns have a lot of houses for sale or rent, but they are all too expensive for homeless people.

Some charities help homeless people to find cheap housing where they can look after themselves.

CASE STUDY

The charity Shelter has offices around the country which help homeless people with their housing problems. Shelter helped Neil get a flat of his own where he is very happy.

Look in newspapers and estate agents' windows to find out the price of houses in your area. How much do they cost?

How would you manage living on your own? Do you know how to pay for the lighting and water in your home? Or how to change a plug? These are things you need to know when you grow up.

NCH Action for Children supports young people who have to leave home and live on their own.

If you don't have a family or friends to help you, leaving home and living on your own can be very lonely and difficult. This is why some people become homeless in the first place. They cannot cope on their own.

Some charities help people learn how to look after themselves, so that they do not end up homeless. Others use some of their money to build low-rent houses and flats to help prevent homelessness.

What would you find most difficult if you lived on your own?

CASE STUDY

Clare used to live on her own and found it very hard to cope. She now lives in a flat provided by the charity MIND. Clare lives by herself but sees a member of staff every day to help her. Without this help she could have ended up sleeping on the streets.

Christmas is often a very lonely time for homeless people. They do not have a home, or a family to share their holidays. With little money, it is hard for them to enjoy themselves.

Crisis Christmas shelters provide warm beds, Christmas meals and the chance to make friends and be with other people.

Every year, the charity Crisis runs shelters during the seven days of Christmas week, so that homeless people can enjoy themselves and be well cared for, just like everyone else.

'What a wonderful Christmas. I'll remember it for years to come,' said Maureen, who is homeless. 'The food was great and we all had such a good time.'

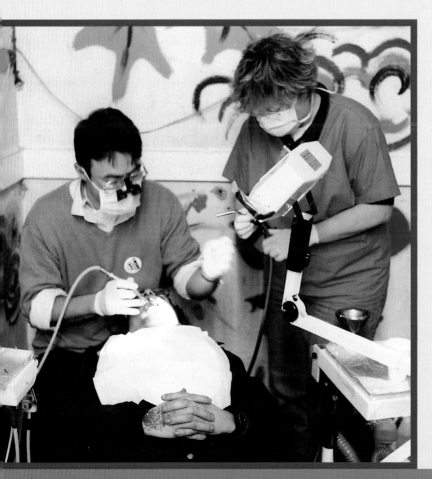

Clothes, hairdressing and medical care are provided by thousands of volunteers, who give up their time over the holidays to help.

Charities are able to help others, because they are given money. This money is given by **governments**, businesses and people like you and me. Together we raise millions of pounds for charity each year.

The easiest way to help charities is to put money in a collection box.

There are many fun ways to raise money for charity. It doesn't matter how silly or simple the idea is - as long as it helps. You could have a cake or toy sale, a bike ride or a **sponsored** silence at your school.

Charities use adverts to show how hard it is for homeless people to survive, and what needs to be done to help them.

This is what you gave in London last Christmas. But your gift helped all the other Open Christmas shelters across the country too.

1,065 visited one of the five shelters in London
100 found accommodation through the Crisis resettlement team
450 talked to the Samaritans (16% of them were having suicidal thoughts or were at risk of suicide)
90 visited the drug and alcohol dependency service
878 visited the medical team (20% up on 1998)
152 saw a dentist

All Jane wants for Christmas is her two front teeth.

The charity, Crisis, produced this leaflet to show how homeless people need health care, just like everyone else.

How could you help homeless people?

♡ How you can help

Have you ever helped anyone? It can feel good to do something kind and generous. You can help by:

● contacting a charity that you are interested in (see pages 30-31) to find out more about what they do. Many charities have children's clubs that include competitions and games, as well as providing information.

● asking your teacher to get someone from a homeless charity to come and talk to your class.

● treating all homeless people you meet with respect. Homeless people are often treated very badly by others, which can make them feel sad and lose their confidence. They have often had to overcome terrible hardship and problems to survive.

● raising some money for the homelessness charity of your choice on your own or through your school. Get your parent, carer or teacher to contact the charity to find out more.

Glossary

donate   give.

government   the people who make laws and rule the country.

hostel   somewhere to stay for a short time. Hostels vary from clean and comfortable to very crowded, dirty and run down.

refuge   a safe place where people can go to escape danger.

refugee   someone forced to leave their home and find safety elsewhere.

rent   paying a set amount of money each week to live in a house or flat.

sponsor   to support someone by giving them money.

♥ Contact details

All of the charities in this book work hard to help homeless people. Contact them to find out more.

Alone in London service
020 7278 4486
www.alone-in-london.gb.org
enquiries@als.org.uk

The Big Issue Foundation
020 7526 3450
www.bigissue.com

British Red Cross
020 7235 5454
www.redcross.org.uk

Centrepoint
020 7426 5300
www.centrepoint.org.uk

Crisis
0870 011 3335
www.crisis.org.uk
enquiries@crisis.org.uk

Jubilee Action
01483 894787
www.jubileeaction.co.uk

MIND
020 8519 2122
www.mind.org.uk

National Society for the Prevention of Cruelty to Children (NSPCC)
www.nspcc.org.uk
Helpline 0808 800 5000

NCH - Action for Children
0845 762 6579
www.nchafc.org

The Refugee Council
020 7820 3000
www.refugeecouncil.org.uk

Salvation Army
020 7367 4500
www.salvationarmy.org.uk

Shelter
020 7505 4699
www.shelter.org.uk
info@shelter.org.uk
Shelterline (24-hour housing helpline) 0808 800 4444

St Mungo's
020 8740 9968
www.stmungos.org.uk
info@mungos.org

UNICEF UK
020 7405 5592
www.unicef.org.uk

Organisations in Australia and New Zealand

Australian Red Cross
(03) 9345 1800
www.redcross.org.au
redcross@nat.redcross.org.au

Australian Salvation Army
(02) 9264 1711
www.salvos.org.au

Save the Children Australia
(03) 9811 4999
www.savethechildren.org.au
info@savethechildren.org.au

UNICEF Australia
(02) 9261 2811
www.unicef.com.au
unicef@unicef.org.au

Women's Refuge
(04) 802 5078
www.womensrefuge.org.nz
info@refuge.org.nz

♥ Index